KINGFISHER
Larousse Kingfisher Chambers Inc.
95 Madison Avenue
New York, New York 10016

First American edition 1995
2 4 6 8 10 9 7 5 3 1
This selection copyright © Larousse plc 1995
Illustrations copyright © Rosamund Fowler 1995

LIBRARY OF CONGRESS CATALOGING-IN-PUBLICATION DATA
The little book of friendship / compiled by Caroline Walsh:
illustrated by Rosamund Fowler.—1st American ed.
p.     cm.
1. Friendship—Juvenile poetry.   2. Children's poetry.   3. Nursery
rhymes.   [1. Friendship Poetry.   2. Poetry—Collections.]
I. Walsh, Caroline.   II. Fowler, Rosamund, ill.
PN6110.F8L58   1995
808.81'0355—dc20   94-19722   CIP   AC

ISBN 1 85697 536 3

Printed in Hong Kong

# THE LITTLE BOOK OF

# FRIENDSHIP

*Selected by Caroline Walsh • Illustrated by Rosamund Fowler*

Kingfisher

NEW YORK

# Contents

Friendship, a dear balm—
Whose coming is as light and music are
'Mid dissonance and gloom:—a star
Which moves not 'mid the moving heavens alone:
A smile among dark frowns: a beloved light:
A solitude, a refuge, a delight.

PERCY BYSSHE SHELLEY

## ABOUT FRIENDS

The good thing about friends
is not having to finish sentences.

I sat a whole summer afternoon with my friend once
on a river bank, bashing heels on the baked mud
and watching the small chunks slide into the water
and listening to them—plop plop plop.
He said "I like the twigs when they . . . you
        know . . .
like that." I said "There's that branch . . ."
We both said "Mmmm." The river flowed and
        flowed
and there were lots of butterflies, that afternoon.

I first thought there was a sad thing about friends
when we met twenty years later.
We both talked hundreds of sentences,
taking care to finish all we said,
and explain it all very carefully,
as if we'd been discovered in places
we should not be, and were somehow ashamed.

I understood then what the river meant by flowing.

BRIAN JONES

For a companion
On my walking trip . . . perhaps
A little butterfly

SHIKI

Over my shoulder . . .
My friends who followed me were lost
In clouds of blossom

CHORA

13

## Together

Because we do
All things together
All things improve,
Even weather.

Our daily meat
And bread taste better,
Trees are greener,
Rain is wetter.

PAUL ENGLE

15

ISABEL JONES & CURABEL LEE

Isabel Jones & Curabel Lee
Lived on butter and bread and tea,
And as to that they would both agree:
Isabel, Curabel, Jones & Lee.

Isabel said: While prunes have stones
They aren't a promising food for Jones.
Curabel said: Well, as for me,
Tripe is a terrible thing for Lee.

There's not a dish or fowl or fish
For which we wish, said I. & C.
And that is why until we die
We'll eat no pie, nor beg nor buy
But butter and bread and a trace of tea.
(Signed) Isabel Jones & Curabel Lee.

DAVID McCORD

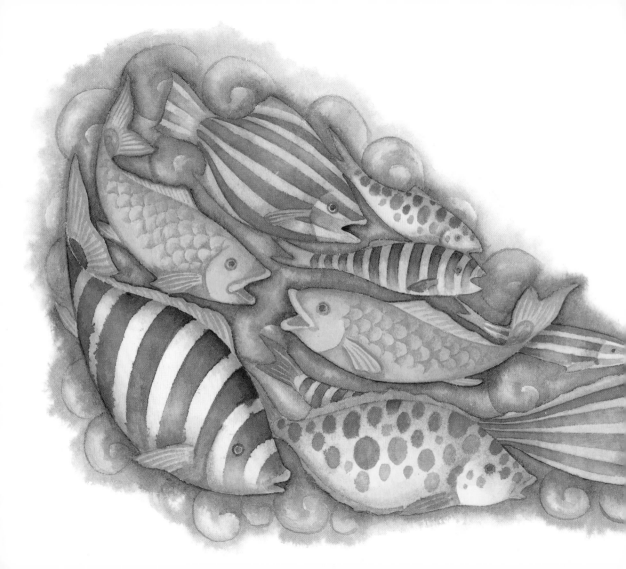

You meet your friend,
    your face
Brightens—you have struck
    gold.

KASSIA

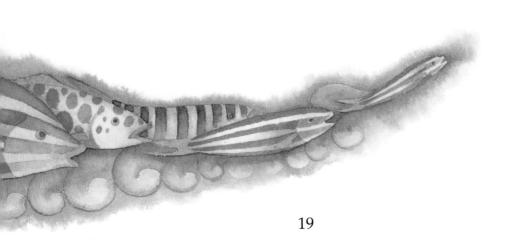

19

## Best Friends

It's Susan I talk to not Tracey,
Before that I sat next to Jane;
I used to be best friends with Lynda
But these days I think she's a pain.

I used to go skating with Catherine,
Before that I went there with Ruth;
And Kate's so much better at trampoline:
She's a showoff, to tell you the truth.

20

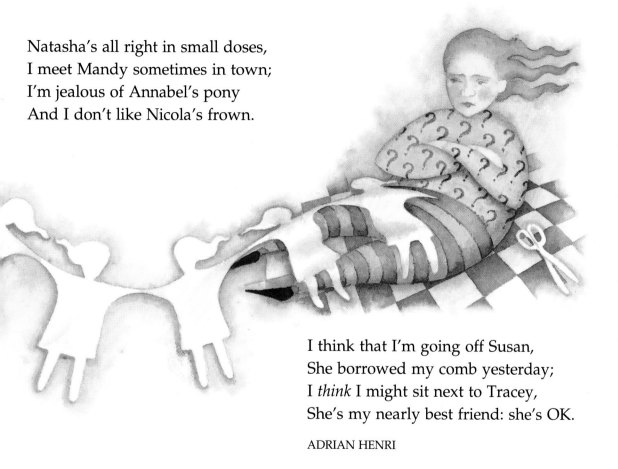

Natasha's all right in small doses,
I meet Mandy sometimes in town;
I'm jealous of Annabel's pony
And I don't like Nicola's frown.

I think that I'm going off Susan,
She borrowed my comb yesterday;
I *think* I might sit next to Tracey,
She's my nearly best friend: she's OK.

ADRIAN HENRI

21

## TRACY VENABLES

Tracy Venables thinks she's great,
Swinging on her garden gate.
She's the girl I love to hate—
"Show-off" Tracy Venables.

She's so fat she makes me sick,
Eating ice-cream, lick, lick, lick.
I know where I'd like to kick
"Stink-pot" Tracy Venables.

Now she's shouting 'cross the street,
What's she want, the dirty cheat?
Would I like some? Oh, how sweet
Of my friend Tracy Venables.

COLIN McNAUGHTON

PUZZLE

My best friend's name is Billy
But his best friend is Fred
And Fred's is Willy Wiffleson
And Willy's best is Ted.
Ted's best pal is Samuel
While Samuel's is Paul . . . .
It's funny Paul says I'm his best
I hate him most of all.

ARNOLD SPILKA

24

## Two Friends

lydia and shirley have
two pierced ears and
two bare ones
five pigtails
two pairs of sneakers
two berets
two smiles
one necklace
one bracelet
lots of stripes and
one good friendship

NIKKI GIOVANNI

## A Good Play

We built a ship upon the stairs
All made of the back-bedroom chairs,
And filled it full of sofa pillows
To go a-sailing on the billows.

We took a saw and several nails,
And water in the nursery pails;
And Tom said, "Let us also take
An apple and a slice of cake;"—
Which was enough for Tom and me
To go a-sailing on, till tea.

We sailed along for days and days,
And had the very best of plays;
But Tom fell out and hurt his knee,
So there was no-one left but me.

ROBERT LOUIS STEVENSON

28

PALS

I'm
sorry for shouting.

Let's
be pals.

I was
wrong the other day.

All
those of
months
being
friends I've startled away,
Like a flock of
frightened birds.

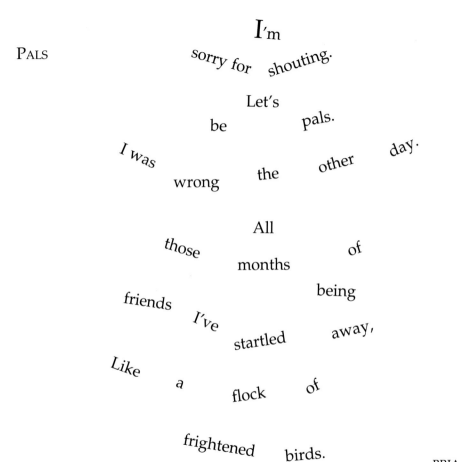

BRIAN PATTEN

## A ROMAN THANK-YOU LETTER

For New Year, Postumus, ten years ago,
You sent me four pounds of good silver-plate.
The next year, hoping for a rise in weight
(For gifts should either stay the same or grow),
I got two pounds. The third and fourth produced
Inferior presents, and the fifth year's weighed
Only a pound—Septicius' work, ill-made
Into the bargain. Next I was reduced
To an eight-ounce oblong salad-platter; soon
It was a miniature cup that tipped the scales
At even less. A tiny two-ounce spoon
Was the eighth year's surprise. The ninth, at length,
And grudgingly, disgorged a pick for snails
Lighter than a needle. Now, I note, the tenth
Has come and gone with nothing in its train.
I miss the old four pounds. Let's start again!

MARTIAL
Translated by James Michie

33

An open foe may prove a curse,
But a pretended friend is worse.

BENJAMIN FRANKLIN

PIGGY TO JOEY

Piggy to Joey,
Piggy to Joe,
Yes, that's what I was—
Piggy to Joe.

Will he come back again?
Oh no, no, no.
Oh how I wish I hadn't been
Piggy to Joe.

STEVIE SMITH

### THE OPPOSITE OF TWO

What is the opposite of *two*?
*A lonely me, a lonely you.*

RICHARD WILBUR

38

### SITTING ON THE FENCE

"Come sit down beside me,"
I said to myself,
And although it doesn't make sense,
I held my own hand
As a small sign of trust
And together I sat on the fence.

MICHAEL LEUNIG

## THE FRIENDLY CINNAMON BUN

Shining in his stickiness and glistening with honey,
Safe among his sisters and his brothers on a tray,
With raisin eyes that looked at me as I put down my money,
There smiled a friendly cinnamon bun, and
    this I heard him say:
"It's a lovely, lovely morning, and the world's a
    lovely place;
I know it's going to be a lovely day.
I know we're going to be good friends; I like
    your honest face;
Together we might go a long, long way."
The baker's girl rang up the sale, "I'll wrap your
    bun," said she.
"Oh no, you needn't bother," I replied.
I smiled back at that cinnamon bun and ate
    him, one two three,
And walked out with his friendliness inside.

RUSSELL HOBAN

YOUR FRIEND THE SUN

Your friend the sun
came round to call
You kept him waiting
in the hall
And as the afternoon wore on
two—three—four
and he was gone

ROGER McGOUGH

## THE YAK

As a friend to the children commend me the Yak.
    You will find it exactly the thing:
It will carry and fetch, you can ride on its back,
    Or lead it about with a string.

The Tartar who dwells on the plains of Tibet
    (A desolate region of snow)
Has for centuries made it a nursery pet,
    And surely the Tartar should know!

Then tell your papa where the Yak can be got,
    And if he is awfully rich
He will buy you the creature—or else he will *not*.
    (I cannot be positive which).

HILAIRE BELLOC

## My Friend

my friend is
like bark
rounding a tree

he warms
like sun
on a winter day

48

he cools
like water
in the hot noon

his voice
is ready
as a spring bird

he is
my friend
and I
am his

EMILY HEARN

49

## Written In The Album Of A Child

Small service is true service while it lasts;
Of friends, however humble, scorn not one:
The daisy, by the shadow that it casts,
Protects the lingering dew-drop from the sun.

WILLIAM WORDSWORTH

## Our Saviour's Golden Rule

Be you to others kind and true,
As you'd have others be to you;
And neither do nor say to men
Whate'er you would not take again.

ISAAC WATTS

## POEM

I loved my friend.
He went away from me.
There's nothing more to say.
The poem ends,
Soft as it began—
I loved my friend.

LANGSTON HUGHES

TAKING LEAVE OF A FRIEND

Blue mountains to the north of the walls,
White river winding about them;
Here we must make separation
And go out through a thousand miles of dead grass,
Mind like a floating wide cloud,
Sunset like the parting of old acquaintances
Who bow over their clasped hands at a distance.
Our horses neigh to each other
    as we are departing.

RIHAKU
From the Chinese (version by Ezra Pound)

There are gold ships,
There are silver ships,
But there's no ship
Like friendship.

ANON

## Index of Authors and First Lines

# Acknowledgments

For permission to reproduce copyright material, acknowledgment and thanks are due to the following:

Alfred A Knopf Inc. for "The Yak" from *Cautionary Verses* by Hilaire Belloc; Peter Pauper Press Ltd for "Over my Shoulder" by Chora and "For a Companion" by Shiki from *A Collection of Haiku*; Random House Inc for "Together" by Paul Engle from *Embrace: Selected Love Poems by Paul Engle*, copyright © 1969 by Paul Engle; Farrar, Straus & Giroux, Inc for "Two Friends" from *Spin a Soft Black Song* by Nikki Giovanni; Nelson Canada, a division of Thomson Canada Ltd, for "My Friend" by Emily Hearn from *Hockey Cards and Hopscotch* by John McInnes and Emily Hearn. David Higham Associates for "The Friendly Cinnamon Bun" from *The Pedalling Man* by Russell Hoban, published by William Heinemann Ltd; Alfred A Knopf Inc for "Poem" from *The Dream Keeper* by Langston Hughes copyright © 1932 Alfred A Knopf Inc, renewed 1960 by Langston Hughes; Michael Leunig for "Sitting on the Fence" from *Rattling in the Wind*, published by Omnibus Books, Australia; Peters Fraser & Dunlop Group Ltd for "Your Friend the Sun" from *Sky in the Pie* by Roger McGough; Walker Books Ltd for "Tracy Venables" from *There's An Awful Lot of Weirdos in our Neighbourhood* by Colin McNaughton, copyright © 1987 Colin McNaughton; Rogers Coleridge & White for "Pals" from *Gargling with Jelly* by Brian Patten, copyright © Brian Patten 1985; New Directions Publishing Corporation for "Taking Leave of a Friend" by Ezra Pound from *Personae*, copyright © 1926 by Ezra Pound; New Directions Publishing Corporation for "Piggy to Joey" by Stevie Smith from *Collected Poems of Stevie Smith*, copyright © 1972 by Stevie Smith; Marian Reiner for the author for "Puzzle" from *A Lion I Can Do Without* by Arnold Spilka, copyright © 1964, 1992 Arnold Spilka; Harcourt Brace & Company for "The Opposite of Two" from *Opposites: Poems and Drawings*, copyright © 1973 by Richard Wilbur; Harrap for "Isabel Jones and Curabel Lee" from *Mr Bidery's Spidery Garden* by David McCord.

Every effort has been made to obtain permission from copyright holders. If, regrettably, any omissions have been made, we shall be pleased to make suitable corrections in any reprint.